allegiance

made in michigan writers series

general editors

MICHAEL DELP, *Interlochen Center for the Arts*

M. L. LIEBLER, *Wayne State University*

advisory editors

MELBA JOYCE BOYD, *Wayne State University*

STUART DYBEK, *Western Michigan University*

KATHLEEN GLYNN

JERRY HERRON, *Wayne State University*

LAURA KASISCHKE, *University of Michigan*

FRANK RASHID, *Marygrove College*

DOUG STANTON

A complete listing of the books in this series
can be found online at wsupress.wayne.edu

allegiance

POEMS BY

francine j. harris

WAYNE STATE UNIVERSITY PRESS

DETROIT

Library of Congress Cataloging-in-Publication Data

harris, francine j.

Allegiance : poems / by francine j. harris.

p. cm.—(Made in Michigan writers series)

ISBN 978-0-8143-3618-2 (pbk. : alk. paper)—

ISBN 978-0-8143-3619-9 (e-book)

I. Title.

PS3608.A78284A792012

811'.6—dc23

2011030703

Designed and composed by Quemadura
in Apollo and Trade Gothic typefaces

*in memory of mary grace johnson, frank johnson
and david blair*

And the mirages, the
 mirages—

 I knew what they were
yet often

changed my course
 and followed them.

ROBERT HAYDEN

. . . names I called you behind your back,
sour and delicious, secret and unrepeatable,
the names of flowers that open only once . . .

RICHARD SIKEN

contents

jumping in

sift

i am not all water
nor does the cue ball sink me
nor the cowboy rope me, nor the monk
sit through me.

i am a thousand faces at
the bottom of the bottom's gravel. the
sea-sharpened stones that clink and
soundlessly shift
make one.

and
i am not all river
not the sand on the tongue's first someone
or even a falling star.

i am all tooth and nail breaks
that bitter underwater
and a million years of sea-smash
dirt in your eye
to dig out.

i am not all nigger:
a black hole crooning in the night.

a country song in a deep
jukebox
chewed down and rumbling.
so who decides
who belongs here
which tooth should have been kicked out when
which hole ought to be filled. this
is what i think:

every city has a country bar.
i am not always so tough when i walk in.

what is rain to the desert
is just another full mouth in some place like portland.
and i wonder if there are niggers here in oregon.
black-out dolls, wet and papery,
their mouths full of chalk.

and some of you
don't go here, either. looking for ground to settle
or a place to sit that isn't soggy and cold. same here.
everything grows damp, eventually.
anything can fall in.

i can put on a bad face, understand.
i can gunload and prostrate. could swallow you whole in any town.

i could keep from throwing the beer bottle, too.
keep from tearing up the green with my teeth.

but can i keep from being silt
from slipping wherever i go.

and is everything something to rot
for our eyes to wriggle out of?

but, i am not all guilty.
nor can i be all sea.
this is just
a bone song. one we can both whistle along the skin to
in a skulk drag, down

through the rift.

costume jewelry

in a pickup truck he gives you everything:
a topless bikini to swim the river in
a scarlet necklace, and a pink towel
which used to be white, to sit on.

you ask him where's the sun and he brings it
just over the hill, catches your ankle while you run
right after the shallow end, and lands
on top of your topless body. you tell him
you always thought you'd die on a roller coaster,
that's your biggest fear, not this.

not people saying they've seen that necklace
in a junk shop. not people calling him
a backwoods boy under a spitty hiss.

so when he asks underwater
if he can blow in your mouth like a bullfrog,
the river water already full in your nostrils,
of course you let him, both because it's funny
and for the sake of how the back of your throat
feels like it could burn forever.

i live in detroit

she said i live in detroit. and there are no flowers in detroit.
so why would anyone in detroit write about flowers in detroit.

i don't tell her we live under the trees. root up curbs and dam fire hydrants
to water black pansies licked to the sides of popped black balloons in detroit.

i'm smashed with the fish under eastern market. when the flower vendors
douse cement, i'm pollen blown off the backs of butterflies in detroit.

like a lot of flowers, i have split my stem. cleaved into root balls. stuck to sweaty
bus windows. like so much dandelion, i get rinsed down shelter shower drains in detroit.

there are plenty of violets in flophouses. pistils broken open
on forty-ounce mouth lids making honeybees bastards in detroit.

i don't tell her look around you. i don't point out the bottoms of coffee cups
where the city spits iris and scratches the back of your throat in detroit.

i tell her: some of our mothers rescued begonias with cheap plastic planters. preferred
    plants to flower. some of them braided pine into sheets, so we could never sleep
    again in detroit.

i wonder if it counts if i wish for frangipani. when i dream in ten spikes of
    passionflower
to cuff inside my elbow. if i can't leave. is that enough flower grounded in detroit.

when it's time to move

what you'd find buried in the dirt under

charles f. kettering sr. high school

(detroit, michigan)

blood:
soaked and caked on white socks, on blue mesh net t-shirts.
   the band leader's blue baton and drumsticks.
matchbooks' gnarled sulfur spilling over newport cigarette butts.
condoms in a few dull shades. tenth grade chemistry books
   modeling atomic fatty acids.
   half-sucked orange dum-dums tucked under detention slips.
   pictures from *black hair* cut out for pre-beautician consensus.
broken black glitter belts with pink buckles shaped like lips.
candle wax from last year's vigil when
   de'andre "chucky" brown
collapsed in the arms of his teammate. the teammate's shoe prints
rocking back and forth at the vigil, biting his lip.
   pieces of the black rubber mat
   below the entrance way, which we crossed every morning,
   teeth clenched. notes of consent that girls didn't really mean
   and wish they hadn't passed back.
broken teeth. lost retainers. crumpled letters written to counselors and discarded
   for illegible handwriting. phone lists of abortion clinics. deflated

valentine's day balloons with trampled white ribbon.
sales ads on bassinette sets. my first boyfriend's piano scarf.
    a phyllis hyman album cover. the path from the exit door
    behind the school through which certain boys
    would not see certain girls leave. torn-up progress reports.
brass knuckles. two
afro picks on opposite sides of the school. germs on a hall pass
    from a boy holding his crotch.
rusty rebar dust. pigeon bones. stolen phone numbers.
    d.o.t. bus passes from 1960, the year of the groundbreaking.
suspended driver's licenses. broken glasses from ice-packed snowballs.
    unread pamphlets on charles f. kettering, a farmer with bad eyesight
    who invented the electric starter and an incubator for preemies.
possum tails. original scores. crumpled poems written and torched
    detailing abuses. genital fluids. dna. envelopes from letters of acceptance
    to states far away. math teachers' stolen answer keys
torn and burned by cigarette lighters.
cigarette lighters. hundreds of mcdonald's fries containers because they flatten
    easily. weed. imitation diamonds from homecoming tiaras
    encrusted in shit-colored mud. research papers on kettering
    detailing his treatments for
venereal disease
    which involved heating up patients in thermal cabinets
    until their body temperatures fevered at 130 degrees.
teachers' red pen marks on essay papers detailing abuses.
    empty sprint cards. broken cell phones.

a splint a football captain

was supposed to be wearing but decided made him look gay.

a *fat boys* tape. pieces of torn blue-and-white starter jackets

from the way boys wrestled each other to the ground in the spring.

my first poetry journal. pages of its poems

embossed with patterns of early name-brand gym shoes.

crumpled suicide notes written in pencil and scorched with ashes.

lost house keys. pictures of first crushes. bullets.

unpublished articles by frustrated teachers

who briefly looked into research findings,

using the charles f. kettering instrument

of school climate assessment detailing the psychological impact

on students of external stressors normally

associated with adulthood domestic patterns of abuse. fat shoelaces.

bullet casings. a jim beam whiskey flask the old principal ditched

thinking someone was coming.

my last boyfriend's lesson plan elaborately structured on the back of

a comic book. imprints of my mother's modest heel

from crossing the barren frontal square at my graduation.

free press articles on unnamed minors whose bodies were found

in dumpsters near kettering. the crystallized block formed

from the tissue my father handed me at graduation

for tears i couldn't explain.

footing, off guard

it is always your word against authority.

baby. who tipped your head into fluid

headlock. positioned your weight against

the thud of their chokehold. baby.

rash of black river, tunneling up to sky. who

gets to howl. and who gets to mouth you

out. call you fowl.

your heavy brow furled into crags over maestro waters,

thersitical thunder, seems

god always gets away with it. baby. blowback into

ready fists. a rage you won't ever get to swirl

herculean clouds against. empty skies.

a fury full of lightning. you know

the taser. memories of love

come like this and linger electric.

wet, conducting ground.

flashes—cyan / magenta / yellow

1. walk into a hospital room and he's got a phone in one hand, a hand in the air, a blanket across the bag of blood at his waist, fake flowers in a styrofoam cup tipped, lights out, camouflaged cigarette falling from behind nylon petal, close to sunset, curtains drawn, burgundy urine, he's screaming into the phone.

2. walk into a house where the knickknacks have increased, tv screen cools, phone waiting (always waiting) to ring. kittens born long enough ago to swirl around an electronic mother, her side shaved in a long patch around a knotted scar. father says she must know this is her last litter: this time, she doesn't ignore them. the monitor cools and cracks. the buzz of china in the cupboard.

3. walk through a door in a dream with a man to find two white lesbians folded over each other in a chair. it's a house in the northwest. can't see the dark trees lonely in the backyard. put a hand in the man's chest to keep him from coming through the door. but the women stay. they don't acknowledge their visitors.

4. an old neighbor who was young when everyone else was young sits in his window all night. his arms are either muscular or fat. it's hard to say. when the young boys pull up to the curb in a small black coupe, they dump their white bag of styrofoam garbage in the street, rough and slick with tar and waiting to be paved. he leans out the window and says *don't be leaving shit in front of my house.* he can't see the dark telephone pole alone behind him. the boys in the car stop laughing. they pick up the bag and put it back in the car.

5. walk into a chain burger joint and a couple is grey. they hold their ticket in hand and say *what's taking so long* to no one in particular. they say they've been waiting an hour. someone says the microwave is broke. they say *shit, we could have microwaved food at home.*

6. walking across the street, the two women in shorts are what we mean by pretty tough. everything shines. the black silk. the patent leather. the brown calves. knees. the plaited hair. the bullseye watching. the tips of cigarettes. the tight skin over shins. the rings through their lobes.

7. walking onto the porch, there is blue glass in the window and a green owl he made when everyone else was young. when kids joined junior achievement and asked bigger people about swimmobiles and sand at the edge of the city airport parking lot. later, he spat on me.

8. it's been years, in fact—an age. there are women sitting on the front porch in blue metal lawn chairs. they look content. there is a breeze. the windows are down. on the street that is not to be walked down. it's the house that survived the fires, the stakeouts, the accusations, the bodies. not to be walked down. i want to stop the car and from the curb, say it—*jesus, woman. do you know what your sons were?*

9. sitting next to the woman who blames the gunshots on how his mother used to talk about him being the product of a gangbang. says giving him her maiden name let the whole world know he was a bastard. *that has little to do with it,* she replies. *children deserve to know the truth.* then she adds that she didn't

know his mother had been done like that. the woman says *yes, the way she talked about it, everybody knew.*

10. from his bed, he jokes with the nurse about taking his pulse but wanting his phone number. he used to be a pimp. he lost money at it. then there was disease. he requests a table near his bedside and the women in the room scurry. it doesn't matter. it could have been anyone, right? the men carry cell phones. he puts the cradle on the table. mother stands the fake flowers back upright. he makes a request, he's mumbling. the women scurry. i hate baby talk.

11. my father used to hate him even before it needed gluing. i never told him he made it, or showed him the cracks in its green, swollen breast. so, he didn't know. these days, he calls him by his drug lord name. proper.

build us a jesus

would like to first thank god

as if god wanted to be thanked. like god cared
about thank you. like god didn't have a whole warehouse of thank-yous
god could pick up out of god's make-me-a-thank-you box whenever god wanted.
    as if god
cared about your folded hands.

god made those hands, god could make the hands fold up.

like god got you your contract. like god didn't have better things to do.
god isn't, after all, the one who raised you, staying up nights waiting to see
if you get in before two. the clock ticks and god is trying to decide whether or not
to have the next hurricane, the way one may decide whether or not to have the soup.

you must think god is codependent. god can take care of god's self. god has one foot
out the door already cause god is sick of your shit, i'll tell you what.

like god was sitting in the audience wearing god's sexiest dress that god bought
just for this night, just because things have been tense between you
and because god wanted you to know that you're still the one,
the one god's always waiting for to come home with
flowers and say *i'm sorry* every once in a while.
it wouldn't kill you.

but tonight

god'll take you
standing up there on the mike thanking god
before you thank your producers
and give shout-outs in code—

side projects. god understands.
god's not jealous. god

is just happy you remembered
that you'd like to thank god.

god's blushing now.

another finger for the wound

(after caravaggio's doubting thomas*)*

jesus. if i had your hair, i'd lasso helicopters.
i'd bring them to a standstill and lift my head up through the blades.

i'd bash my head into control towers and laugh at all the pilots who bet my scalp.
for me, gravity would turn off its meter and wait, i'd make sure of it.

if i was you, jesus, i'd yell for days. i'd pull the pin
from my mouth and blow up waterfalls
just to hear the glass it breaks. i'd shred canals.
i'd blow holes into eardrums.

if i could glow like that, jesus, i'd flame.

i'd show up in parking lots with moons in my mouth.
stuff eels into my eyelids. i'd roll my own image

like a spliff. jesus, if i was black and you were the dealer,
i wouldn't believe you. you'd have three cards in a monte.

and i would never pick. i'd stand off to one side
and laugh at all the lip-licking believers trying to move their eyes that fast.

i'd keep one trick in my ear. i'd need more proof.
what if you were white on purpose?

let's just say you *were* jesus. then we could tap dance.
we'd shuffle so fast your temples
would look like a top hat

flexing fog.

in the fall, you'd rustle down leaves like tornadoes.
we would wear them on our silver-toed shoes.
i'd wipe the horizon with your laugh line. i think you and i would click.

jesus, if you *were* white, you'd cut your hair pink and be a punk.
you'd feed chlorophyll to gutters under gasoline.

maybe you'd hold my hand.
maybe you'd turn your veins out and show me your junk.
maybe for me, you'd kick.

but you.
you rattle in the dirt to keep quiet.
you hide in the periphery. run from the limelight.

you die in crowds and call us all lost. if you were

really jesus, we'd both be sand travelers. so what if they smirk.
if i were black and you were jesus, we
would eventually switch.

you wouldn't mind my fingers in your gashes, in fact
it wouldn't occur to you to be painted.
you'd understand that people are broke.

you'd rip
your rib from my rib, and together

we'd share the marrow's milk.

the splashing of the bush

(in the midst of the franciscan order—st. aloysius, downtown detroit)

i.

the church has shrunk since i was a kid. the priest

a little fatter. the downtown is desolate coming in. the bus stops
are vacant. there is a woman in an embroidered hat

crossing her daughter. an old man in a belted safari shirt
hands me a program at the door. these days, the priest rocks

to a gospel choir. no one speaks in latin. still, a kneeling woman
rests her hips back into the pew, and i weep for my mother.

this goes on the whole time.

ii.

the priest brings forth four children. his wrists reach into a baptismal urn.
he bunches the roped branches

and heaves them out. red ribbon, wet branches. green shrub leaves, dripping
    water, he swings
the bush over the kids. to remind them,

he says, of their baptism. then, laughing, he walks the bush down the aisles,
    swinging
the splash over the crowd. the crowd lifts their faces to lap at the water, crossing

wet foreheads, crossing our wet chests. i like
he is smiling.   the way his cheeks rose.

   iii.

i like

holding hands with the man next to me. he is blond and his skin is blond.
    his hands
are average and warm, and i cannot hear him sing as we

forgive those who trespass against us (my mother sung horribly. switched from
    soprano
to baritone mid-song)

and lead us not i pulse my fingers in the blond's palm.
into temptation he pulses back.

iv.

from the gospel according to john, father todd tells us there were those
who doubted jesus. they said:

just show us the father.

he says *haven't you been with me, all these years. look at me, and you see the father.*
    jesus

and i would have been introduced several times. i would have found him
admirable. the way you have to admire

a pimp. when another person would introduce us, jesus would wink at me and say

yes, i believe we know each other.

v.

kneeling is my favorite part. kneeling, and the blood and
body. the literal blood and body. i argue

with myself why i should be able to take communion. i want
to drink christ's blood, eat

from his chest, his arms, his tendons. they say it will get me
closer to heaven. so then let it. i weep for wanting

jesus, the pimp. how secretly, everyone wants
to be turned out. jesus

could lift the shirts of desert men, hearts writhing for his
silk-stained chest. rising and falling. sweat

catching the light of the stars.

vi.

       compositionally,
father todd's tonsure leads the eye

to a gilded shepherd, st. francis, hoisted high on the wall.
my body would look good there, too

hung.

vii.

what if we could discuss the passions. father todd
would have to be naked.

viii.

there's a family in the pew in front of me.

they have two little girls. one white. one who looks bengali, and her hair is
   cropped short like mine. father todd says *let us pray.*

the church falls silent and holding on to the wooden pew in front of her, the
   bengali girl cranes her neck. over father's neck and head. over the gilded
   francis. over the murals reaching the ceilings.
under the unused

pipe organ, until her eyes meet mine, upside down. she

watches, watches, watches
my wet eyes. she

tries to wink.

ix.

the old man in the safari suit touches my back. *aren't you going to take communion.*

x.

i wink back.
　　she tries again.

lost pen

confessional poetry

you are a thousand priests. a sea of priests. the human priest. i beg your forgiveness.
i beg it long winded. i beg with no form. i beg insurrection. i beg the resurrection.
do you have

the time for this   priest. will you hold my head up   priest. father. is it quiet there.
are there grasses. is there mud. i love the way you touch my hair. i love the way you
us, us sinners. i got your edits, did you get my *our fathers.* please don't throw out
the baby water. please don't let the pews be empty. the drip white candle, burn til
she bows. cheap for a votive, burn til she blows. goddammit the lattice. father *hail*
marys. sometimes i forget my poems. bless me father, i don't remember my lines. it's
been this since. since the sin. this is my last confession. (once a priest told me

he forgets his sermon. *bless me sinner, for i cannot haunt.*) i beg you hold your head
up steady. you'll tell me if you forget your glasses. did you only come for wine. then
drink the wine, and take this priest. drink the words, and open priest. drink my
sins, and bathe me priest. i only come for your drummer's ear.

your forehead is the colored glass light. i'm your kneeler, i fall when you joke. your
kneeler thuds the ceramic floor. your kneeler studded, your mouths in smiles. your
mouths to throat. your starlight cheek. you smile of priests. touch me where there's
nowhere priest. hear me out. take me in and pull the curtain. you're a hollow priest,
my sorry soul.

                                                                    i need this pen.

get me to god.

somewhere outside acme,

i believe in castles.

a story of lions. a wish on silver. oriel windows, and a body i know well in
chiffon. why do my fantasies make the laurel ornate. decorations on every

little girl wish. why not some sensible plan for castle acquirement.
        english inheritance. i have a tigress in my hair

        and linden in my collarbone. for god's sake, enough
with my detroit brain. click myself lakeside.

undress in white beach three times. salt
        my shoulders with ocean. gut

        fish with flints of mica. i
could have it. so tell it

to my nights.

choosing poets, out of town,

like choosing a date

never use love in a song.
but never is long.
and always just as wrong.
—pure horsehair

number one reminds you of staring at video boxes and dreaming in new york. how you pack up all your black-and-white photographs and move to new york. chop off your hair instead of getting some dumb tattoo. his face is quarter-cropped in the camera box and you can imagine drinking with him by a dumpster. in the second poem, he mentions rats, and you think of the rats whose glare you tried to return in the subway. how it was like they were waiting for something. he's good at these words and they look like sticky stars on the tops of new york skyscrapers. he is as wiry as the nervous boy who sat next to you for both semesters of shakespeare. but it is like he is waiting for you to fall off the platform. no one makes such pretty discoveries this consistently. the you who would buy this book really wants to be lied to.

number two takes on rebellion, but renders it in the colors and tin tunes of a circus. corners, with him, you would take on new limbs. he reminds you of boys who never told you their secrets, but who would wear your eyeliner in public, on a dare. you probably share the same myopia, but he has adjusted to the strain. you might both breathe hard at the same altitude in the northwest, but in the misty mountain rain, he knows how to swerve a squirrel on a winding road. he has a billy tuft of hair under his lip—it all seems metaphysical. he graffiti sketches flower bombs on warehouse walls and rides the ferry to bainbridge to twirl fire with his friends on their organic farms. you'd buy him for the same reason you started hiking, for fear of the dirt. he might make your body wilt the right way, but he's also too good at making things. you'd both supine mumble at each other. there's a natural oat to his fingertips. he says *tell me* and doesn't mean it. it is your job to say it just right, so you leave the wild wheat in his eyes.

but number three. well, number three lives in alaska. his picture makes you sad. he reminds you of the men you shot pool with in phoenix. who rented rooms by the week. who only stopped smiling long enough to get down a shot. who tried hard not to mention their ex-wives. who tucked in their black rock band t-shirts. whom you didn't fuck, and who didn't ask. in their motel rooms, legal papers littered their shelves propped up by cinder blocks. you could always smoke in their rooms.

his name is joseph. his hair is parted asymmetrically, which seems to have something to do with what you've already lost and what you think you will never find again. of lake towns, like this one, where women's bellies emerge and slip out from under not-so-feminine khaki. of women who barely flick an eye over their velcro dress straps. this one walks the cold beach, but the fugue is soft. joseph. the babies his book wants to seep from young girls and their pine-tall stances. the men, expectant worriers, who hold up their women in line for coffee. the perfume of wide-band miniskirts wash down the sandstone wall.

joseph . . .

lay back alaska. run through its strong bays. the couples here bow to the weather. in summer, they share gelato from a green cup. but in winter, they will sip ice from one another's teeth. someday, visit yourself here with me in our new town. the cold doesn't seem to bother you, so i think we could love anything. the setting sun will cut up these women's mouths and then we can set it all out to freeze.

we could carry our guns together. we would stink of the smoke from burning the weekly trash. our bodies would grow hair underwater and the contrast would curl into seaweed and sharks.

which you would skin. and lay the bones into flaccid bells. clink, *to alaska*. to alaska missing its scales. before skin could

smoke, he might find a wolf under my knees, and i might be wearing his pants. memories would ellipse and slap at our eyelids. we would snore and tell no one. no one to tell.

joseph with the piercing alaska, yes.

our feet are turning white.

there is always someone.

that's the problem.

here comes the mailman.
fuck his footsteps.

in the scheme of things, none of these leaves
help the aching bone in my foot.
so fuck the leaves.

fuck the leaves. fuck 'em.
when they sog up in the rain and forget about
who has to rake them up.
fuck the ruckus they cause up under the snow. fuck

how horny they seem, all wet. how they prop up
on one elbow. how dark, here at the bus stop
like i should take them home.

i wish it were this simple.
i'm not blind, or fucked, and fuck them for knowing that.

i wish the leaves would get down on one knee. repeat after me.

i wish the leaves would get down on one knee

and kiss this heat.

i wish i didn't have to believe in sound like they don't have to believe in sound.
it's not snowing yet. and i wish my body would soften.
words, i wish for them too.

the daylight thinks this is funny. tells you to sleep it off.
        yeah, well.

fuck him too.

why i haven't written

because there's a storm coming and nothing to say
and the paper shortage and the last time
we opened windows   from the fever, until daybreak
                    and the house was dirty
                                        and we were snowed in
          and we wondered how close we really were and we said, *let's wait and see.*

nothing worth being new.   since you married, we only speak
of road trips the way one pretends to remember the cross streets of gory accidents
          aside from chatter about old friends (who also haven't written) because

i loved you, the way only a coward can, head cocked and hands out
          and because to write would be to bring up the dusky sunset where there
used to be a carnival
every spring for the neighborhood kids. now it's an empty lot.

and i haven't written you
          because you raised me, and to write would be to traipse a barbed wire
                    across distance, admit it
would be to erect a cage
          to show off what we can't say.
the days you once woke me
          in winter, before school,
are over, and without them   we are failing.

all of this, i told you the last time i wrote, from the last state,
that i wouldn't write in case of war, should i suddenly feel
ashamed, and turn up gathering in mobs, or joke about needing
evidence of good people. script gets to be a parasite
looking for soft spots in the skin.

and i haven't written you
because we are still sharing handfuls of licorice,
and you stick around until it's gone, and in my head
it's all over everything while we sort through boxes of old journals, find
space to walk in, the leap of years.

if i wrote, i would need a thousand days for one
to fret that place to place, the pickup in your names turned to echo,
a pollen carried like a praying mantis in white sheets
beneath the desert blades of a fan. and to write
when the fuse blew would be to turn it with my hands.

i used to write

and later they told me you couldn't read them.

       if you got it, if you begged teachers to show you,

it didn't stop the way they tracked you, or teach you how to read. which does make
   me wonder

        what became of our countless excuses for contact, the dime store flower fields

you never got.   the ones i would walk three blocks to mail

                      to a boy across the street.

i wonder what became of the times when i did write

         and if you knew that in all those notes,

     from report backs on diamonds at summer camp

to the long-winded streams over ice ponds,

that every letter was always the same letter

        with the same hope that we would keep them.

and if i haven't written, it's only because things

           have become somewhat more permanent.

wear metal

intention

the morning's alarm is shrill. the sky
blue for birthing. a brightness intended
for violins. how could the harbor be squeezed

into a bird on a ledge. contrast, the candle

against day. fizz of light's arc shadow through
the hollow wall, the window. such clarity has brought

down planes. has committed people to dungeons.
the diligence of sun rays. the hovering glass.

the bright eye peaks at light. a vinyl shiver.
light on the morning disappears
clock faces. morning

reaches to engulf.

(i belong to that voice.

it owns what i breathe.)

if inside writhing sirens, a man screams and is licked alive, then i say open your arms. press your breadth against the confines of their forms.

let 'em know. don't just stand there full of branches and mouths. your body is a linger. your fragrant words, siphoned. use your mouths, for godsake. any of them. though i was ready with brass, i never was a grace note.

we said *who cares*.

i don't just wish you the hollow of give-anything-soothers who keep their mouths caved open. i wish it for me, too.

their backs turned to your eyes, so you watch without me. lightning. there's enough to fill the whole sky. your eyes

still the jetty night's tide. who do i think i am.

> *coda*
>
> exit from under my breast the way you came.
> say my name on the way out.
>
> i'll suffer the rib being ripped to milk.

bitch take it.

without me, there's plenty to watch. woe is my sex. all tall and spilling coneflower. woe is everything we sweat out and walked off smoking and ripping out walls and couching *i love yous* in knuckles dragged along cement.

tell me, *ever.* don't say ever, then—even if you're referring to the way the horizon sucks back its own tongue of ocean. salt-filled, its one good eye, its very own morbus.

don't even say you mean it. let that be the ever we end on.

fume

love is a rage that never quite slaughters. a murder with no body. a lighthouse
    sinking invisible ships. a robber with no hands.

a rapist alone.   love is a room with
                                no doors, no windows, one chair and a rope.
                          it's a missing item in a missing stack. a skin
                          that won't sink to the bullet. love
                          is too tight.
it breaks.
    it's a toilet filled with latex gloves. a burn on the stomach you don't remember.
                                    it opens your fly every time it pees. love
                                         doesn't
                                         pick
                                         up
                                         on
                              body language.
  it pulls your panties down in an unfinished basement. it kisses your eyelid with
                                         crap
                                       in its
                                  tooth. love

           trails off in a long,
               ragged
wheeze. it rips your lips in church.
it talks too damn much.

love faints giving blood, but it keeps giving blood. it's the stranger you let in to use the phone. it purrs at your feet, but it has those claws. it's the way you feed and the leash you toss.

it scratches in the walls.

you, old meany

after allen ginsberg's "america" . . . **long after**

detroit, every time you open your mouth, my cheeks get frosty. detroit, you've got
a bad habit of spitting when you talk.
i know you're gonna get me, i hear you coming in my sleep. detroit, when will
your bald incense men stop leaving their limp penises on my voicemail.
detroit, you killed my parents. this is not funny. detroit, i didn't even mean to start
off like ginsberg. but maybe you're the reason i cried when he died. he knew
he'd never leave. smoking and sweating and stuck with leftover cum in his ass.
detroit, i've got your construction dust in my brassiere straps. your bus drivers
snarl at me when i ask about connecting stops, i'd rather drive. detroit, your
good bartenders have gunk in their throats.
detroit, the women too. detroit, the women too don't get to wear our short skirts
unless we've got a man on our hip. detroit, you take my men and hurl them into
starry existential brain farts.
detroit, you act like your maniacs are admirable. detroit, you sit and fart on your
intellectuals and suggest they do more slam poems.
detroit, for the last time, i don't want to go to church. i've been to church, it hurts
my knees. detroit, at church, you give me a cracked body of christ and herpes
in plum wine. detroit, at church i get hungry for the wafer and the wine and i
want to go drink with mean women who write strong beer poems, but there are
none. they all live in krakow.
detroit, your breath stinks. it stinks of cursing out too many gas station attendants

and employing mexicans and calling them mexicans. detroit there's no lysol for
this, it's in your lungs—snow poisoned the color of monoxide.

detroit, you don't take your snow seriously. detroit, i take your snow seriously and
i would love to put your flakes inside my thighs sometimes, but your snow
won't have me but on some ole pimps-and-hoes–type shit.

detroit, why do you raise up hoes out of your girlchildren singsonging lyrics in
pink leg warmers and stiletto boots. detroit, why am i jealous of your pole
dancers.

detroit, your pole dancers have nicer asses than i do and your seats are made to fit
them.

detroit, i've gotten off my point. detroit, you used to call me mean and look at the
foam around your nasty mouth. detroit, you've got a pinched nerve and i'm
sitting all over it. detroit, landmines made out of glass bottles, loose pit bulls
and rottweilers pulling little boys down van dyke.

detroit, you reek of factory sulfur. your rust belt is choking my mood. detroit i
wheeze your diesel, where should i move. detroit, you cradled me with your
smog and cement through all my temper tantrums, who will choke me with
such tender particulate matter.

detroit, can you please fuck me back once in awhile and then we can talk. detroit,
no one's listening anyway. i've got a bump in my chest that moves up and down
while i sleep.

detroit, i still love your red throat pheasants. they seem so content to roam on
awkward toes and end up finding nothing.

detroit, you're gonna take me for granted on the wrong day, i can be mean too.
detroit, stop telling me this is my fault. i'm just a fucking zygote trying to see
you, so i know what to look like.

detroit, take off your clothes and come to bed.

three feet of

personal space

one's nature

this box is a box. you watch the box, to see if the box moves. because it is a smart box, a box with good form, you think it may transcend its boxiness. still a box. the worst kind of box—boxing up all boxes. you watch the box to see if the box will elongate, or sickle. it could, after all, shoot at crests or do something equally parabolic. if the box could gripe of gross negligence, the box would tell you—it has seen a tangent. it knows what it lacks. the box would be the first to tell you it's not the brightest bulb in the box. in fact, due to the box's sun sign, the box considers triangles the most formidable of configurations. they never take any mess. always on the move. never well, ya know, lonely. the box has scooted over from time to time, allowing room for other boxes. but this may not be clear, as there seem to be sides laying around everywhere. then again—not the tidiest of boxes. consider this, box could have come in any shape or plane. when it hurts, blade. when it simpers, peanut. but a hurting box must remember that in the life of a box, a sort of shaved feeling comes with having one side exposed all day, from being the very box that is stored inside the box's own head. the box blinks. folds. a corrugated nerve center has recommended this as a form of transcendental polygonal breathing. so it blinks and folds. blinks and folds. and we would never call the box suggestible. we would only say the box is a box. that's what they do.

to the man on the bus

i don't like your mouth. i don't like the crusty edge, or how it looks like it smells.
i don't like that it won't stay still.

there's something goddamn about that mouth.

you don't even deserve it.

you who plays with popsicle sticks.
who rides the bus with a bloody crack in your lip.
you even have a cell phone ring that's ridiculous.

every time i think it's dry, you start it all over again.

and i hate those caps you wear. i don't like the way you sit.
your fanny pack. your dirty brown bag. i don't like the mustard stain you leave
whenever you switch seats.

i'm not saying your mouth isn't full of things i could like.
it is full of things i do like,
like lampposts and cracked teeth
and the word *fucker*.

once, some little girl put a fatty nipple on that lip.
is that what made it crack? you were young then.
i hate you anyway.

i could just say *you've opened your mouth for the last time.*

but i've already opened my mouth.
i already lied about who i am.

you can't remove the city

but you can use all the words you know. the tense you can conjugate. you can put the concrete in the image. the back of the bone is what you say behind the crack of your teeth. that is your only plausible tongue. the city won't translate it for you. to rename any of these words constitutes betrayal. you'll get it cut off. get it gouged out. don't dare make this a junkyard, where the teeth empty out refrigerator motors, where they lay stabbed and cut up. their puffy corpses all along lawnmower yards. someone at this point will undoubtedly point out the heidelberg. and they will think it is the only art here that ever burned at the stake, got murdered on the sidewalk by too many colors. this city sky. here, at the bus stop, tell 'em. capitol park is touching you. it parts your ankles dirty. it is stuck in the oil between cornrows. here is your three-ring griswold and washington. it smells of vaseline. you miss your father, don't you. this city spit him up.

crooked teeth

senses

black uniforms scold
sun, unstitch its field-rough gold.
fences yield to sleep.

> watch nights. be a hawk.
> sharpen wood's warp to a rust.
> give the mouths their say.

children, cicada.
hydrant beats and sticks, summer
scorches old fight dogs.

lots bloom rat suckle.
urine stuck to sugar glass.
plumes of hyacinth.

blackberry sidewalks.
palmers in the comb, strippers.
party store snow cones.

bricks of a bruised skin / walls where pipes bend like bear tongue / snow tans a deep hide

what teeth poems ain't

i have no time to tinsel my poems. no water to wet them with. they dry out under dangling wires. they are middle-aged magicians, touching. what if their hands were sweaty. what if they both had strokes. these poems will never sell.

sometimes, these poems wish they hadn't come. they sit in the corner and hope no one will notice them digging in their nose. they still like to talk, but they twitch. they pretend no one can see them scratching. they sweat lip strangers who give them the pity "hi." they ramble on and aim for clever, because they remember once when they were clever. they hold a quiver lip steady and watch people turn to leave.

sometimes these poems lie. they look people straight in the eye and say they were never born. they buckle under the weight of river bridges. because it's dark and smells warm, these poems look for a moss they can feel. they suck the mold deep into their gums, where a mold can multiply. these poems break their teeth on concrete, to see if it's the teeth that bleed.

these poems are cheats. they light too many votives for a quarter. they tell lies in confession and take two turns. they hide names and make up facts. they steal colored light bulbs from classrooms. they take the comfy pillow. they avoid eye contact and sit up straight to hide hand-drawn porn. they shoplift lip gloss.

these poems are malnourished. their hair is thinning. they suck on whitening strips, but no teeth. you could find these poems in thrift stores. they're no good dog food. cheap crazy glue. dull childproof scissors. they break off wood for walking sticks. then sit the whole thing out.

documents

a goat's blood

                                          is a document. and a hoof hungers here

as it swats in the dark, folds to its own

        bellies, carves at its own restless intestines, which attract

                                    the carrion, yes, but also the bees,

which stick

        in the ear. and stuck in the ear, can't shake with a finger.

               or cotton. or oil. and when the vertigo drops through the floor,

                              these are the falls

and the bodies that blur

        the bodies abandoned. these are the corpses, too,

which are the same bodies, fixed and fixed

        until covered in scabs.

        itched to a tender.

                which these fingers pull

           and anoint and peel

        again to the quick.

never had to use a gun

neighbor

sometimes this city doesn't talk. there's always someone
across the street chewing down a toothpick.

here it seems everyone always has more than you do.

more money, more hoes.

more desire inside his mouth full of chipped teeth.
more ways to suck sap from tree bark.

more desire to drink, than to talk about it.

from the bottom

i submit because it would be a mess and kind of animal.
i would like the bone shards in my cheeks.
i submit because

i would walk away in tears. because
they always win, so fuck it.
it's better to have to lick up your fingers
than to have to lap up the floor.

i submit because i like to leave them intact.
i know the feast in their eyes. i respect it, no.
i'm famished.

i submit because i can't see the spot on the floor to kneel.
i know how the knees can beg. i know what a hard floor can do.
i get the difference when the weather aches. i know altars and pews

and how trains leave on hard gravel. i know men's basements.
i know how to leave on the lights.

i submit to keep from being talked out of my spine.
never let the mess of a beggar's please. i submit
and let them rest their case.

i submit to study the look on their faces.
they like to see what they're getting. cities
of men cock their heads in the light. below the ceiling

it's always there.

and i watch from below to see when it changes. i watch to wait
for the noise in their throats. i know how to grieve, but

i submit so the last word is tucked in my shirt.

you don't have to come up with
anything. you don't have to react.
all you have to do is disappear.

the road to jackson has orchids

i need a man that's just been stabbed,
fresh out of prison.
i want a christian non-smoker.
—call in to radio show . . .

walked
this road plenty times, never thought to sniff for flower, wish
we could someday edge the yards from here to the county line.
wonder what machine could do it, stubble in the mouth, shave the
lawn so i'd just walk out the backdoor and be here, shaved. done it
a thousand times to make it worth it. count how many times you
shave a year then, a lifetime of razor blades come too close, who first figured out
the angle, troubled the equation, or the likelihood, to a promise not to draw blood,
who was the first throat, or the first skin, did ladies shave their legs when there were
strops, did barbers do their wives' bikini lines, whip up lather and sharpen the blade
to get between the ass. a fine angle and a bird that smells like a car on fire.
grease and gasoline to cook it on a cement slab, just up the road now, a bit
further. put the cap on and let it burn. slow with a knife around just in case.

when they let me in, do i take my bra off. do i promise not to do him,
do i say *ma'am* and *sir*, what if they make me bend over, what
if they put a hand down my blouse. do i show them this license,
where i stuck out my tongue at the clerk and anyway, she took

it, didn't say *please give us a straight face, ma'am.* is that
contraband. if i bring orchid, they'll probably confiscate it.
should of picked a rose. roses are the standard.
hope he doesn't cry too much when i tell him.
we're pregnant again. god willin' he'll get to
hold her by the time she's walking.

rub against it, where

it fills your mouth like gum.
    and pulls the roof to tongue.
    and bad shapes your teeth to soothe. say *no*
    until it falls off your bike like a chain
        and catches in the spokes. fall on its groan like a hard pillow.
    like a spike, the belly. fall on it
        like the boy you said it to, then ever stuttered after.
        knock your forehead against its forehead. chip
    its own tooth. say it
    until your hands itch from saying it. say *no*
    until you lose friends for saying it. until
        its bridge
breaks and thousands fall
    from its ropes. say *no*
    until everybody drowns who can't swim in it. say it
        until you're one of the drowned.
until your bodies
    decompose under the river and blue. until
    its machines pull all of you into its metal chains. say it
while the oil fills your spines with salt. say it
    while the air lifts geese, indifferent. say it
    until your own jaw is slack
        and the spittle falls long like a sad drool in a pool
        of *no*. say it

to god. ask why your mouth is filled

      with lumps of *no*, rocks of *no*, silt filament

filling your lungs of *no*.   *no*

      to the bugs and the fish.

      no to ten boggy fingers.

          say it to the crust rib, the thick, drenched scar,

      the thump of the sunken breast.

          say it

until every part of you can shatter bone.

      until there is enough cold locked inside you

          to thaw a black fog.

sit with you all night

midday nap

the grits what made me sleepy, stuck
and settled over skin-slipped tomatoes and ground up salt.
swollen pepper beast fat over breakfast, i thought we were starting the day.
and all that grease and wither is just a matter of facing up
to what we didn't have the guts for yesterday. the gnash teeth,
the open doors. fifty pigeons line up to break their beaks
on dog food in the backyard, push around with their bodies
and the long straw of arched black eyes, i thought

we would get up, and then take care to push off
extra covers, sag pillows, shove them off into the attic window
say whatever it takes to let the plates cake in their place
fattened on meatless sludge, the starches glued
our teeth so we chew on it. say we thought
there was more to do. maybe shutting in is
some kind of day already set.
crows in the yard take up where the pigeons left off.
couldn't get beaks in the machine-fused pebbles.
they're the smart ones. they advertise the sky.
the busy keep on coming.

feeder

take this belly and sit it out to collect rain.
let the critters swarm in it. let it make islands of milk for a cat's mouth.
they like it fresh, while it still moves. you should know this.
for birds, roll the meal into grub.
perch it on that fence you love.

go ahead. make an old woman's morning.

eventually butterflies. the usual orange stampede. taste the blackberry thorn.
set the moth's tongue toward tomorrow. every hot light gets
afraid of tomorrow, doesn't it. until it turns. then

squirrels. fat tails swat off a cat's bloated jowl. thick up
the puddle with hair. with browning. with noon. gradually, snails

mosquitoes, body plumped of blood. swirl down the sun.
nothing here is promised. but we've already committed

evening. didn't even know it. shaved pine shells. centipedes.
and the inverse arch of my belly left out, cockroaches begin again.

free it up
so the swarm knows how to proceed.

should it wait until the next rainfall.
should it wait at all.

until it comes

nothing to say is a floor full of black mouth.
the black of crayons inside thick, grey sleeves.

memory drips black custard on the floor, or dollops of dead black hair.
done in the dark. done with a handful. done inside a fist.
done in black bulbs and blown out black tufts of air
a deep yonder of tar. it leaves its bodies strewn.

nothing left to say is loose mud kicked off
from children who try their words on
like shoes—over and over again. it's a tease.
a torture.

you used to punch holes through your lips to get at the words.

now, you're all nod black alley.
you're all rained out diamonds
mumbling the grey wax of a song you forgot.

your head opens grey
and black ash puffs and can't breathe.
you're wearing your nothing black mask.

nothing is taking cover on a ball field.
is dodging the spoken draft.

nothing words are thickening into a syrup
ripe for yellow jackets.

something in the water

maybe today the woman
who walks her dog will just walk her dog. maybe wet
she'll walk her dog wet, as fat as she was
yesterday, but you won't have to say *fat*
or *wet dog* or anything at all.

you may be tempted to say *gee, that's a . . . mighty big dog* but maybe
the skin and the bark and the drops and the hair
will walk the day
without it.

maybe today, you'll just see a woman walking
or a form moving. or a dog in a form
or a form in the rain. maybe
today you'll sit and not have to say
anything at all.

whoever sits next to you will have to
go un-entertained. her form
will form her form
in falling forms, and your mouth

will make no empty shapes
on air.

parturient

must mean a kind of heat that moves ants through the blood
in search of sugar.

rinse
      and they return. now you see
      their bodies flicker, suck sweet flake skin
      from the tops of their heads

in all this green grass. it must mean they will find you.
                      maybe they name and map you.

only when desire drags your knees over rocks, and the blood is outside
                      are you spared.
      only with petals' swell will the throb
      throw out everything. replace the itch.

      note : nothing eats
      an altar.   nothing knows how to wreck

its dust. the fragrant insect instead, genuflects.

it must be the line people faint out of.
a minnow's shadow
      when you can no longer see the fish.

it must mean bridges that sweat thickets and
     murderers who sit with their palms turned up.

but there is no word for this.
     in the clearing, consider how everything changes
    should you betray love.

       you are a wetland, capable of bogs.
you are a sudden cliff.

they seem to gather

in one park

i wanted you so i parked by the acorn trees
under the aculeate sky.

instead, i tucked music
into jacket pockets, headphones.

wanted you and walked
the breeze in the shape of bees.

i fed ice from my cup instead
to the sand and soaked the playground.

i wanted you. so i put my tongue
to the trees and tasted yellow jacket.

instead i ran from the stingers
and sat in the shade.

i wanted you. and i touched my throat
where honey, where a girl.

instead, i beat all the kids
to the slide in my dirty skirt.

i did want you. i picked acorns
fat as greek olive. wizened wing.

i separated caps from their jade bodies.
i let them die out in the sun.

between old trees

there's a rain formed. it has a face that reminds you

of hills. it has a country you could name if you were smarter.
it has a kind of mouth. it seems wrecked from all the commotion
of a windstorm. it has tear ducts, and what does that say about
you. it lives by the hope that someday again there may
be bluing in a backyard wash, so far off
the sky. this is why children
chalk suns on the sidewalk. the wind brings north
through a hundred miles
of inanimate things.

when it hits, all the places you have been
seem too late to talk about. all is grey
that storms, and it crosses the country on busses,
looks for burned trash, hopes to see enough rivers,
hums something you can't quite remember
but still you sleep. still, you wear no shoes
against the pavement and sometimes
the lightning, sometimes a wet rail
you lean over, and ruin your only pants.

addicted to addict

dickhole and denise

he ran black circles around the tub
and called to her.

porn face, come in. let me rub your shoulders
with scissors. let me drip water on your staple so you rust.
the half-baked light flattens your tit, let me lick my brain.

he farts. a long bubbling fart and her nose
doesn't light up, her veneer isn't startled.

let me see your twat. the glassy juice frozen in time
like everglades, like a slurpee melt. a blueberry yum.
you would taste of mango. he scrubs underneath one nut.

let me stab you into closet spaces. let me hack off
the porker stabbing you in your mead gutter. let me razor him
out at the nub. oooo. it's still in you. let me try to fix that.

the fuck furl in her brow has not changed. she does not
ask her friends if this is normal.

oh. the scissors won't reach. i'm sorry. let me please
stick my polepopper up in your caveplanter in my head.

he folds back one leg and cuts out another munchpot
to position directly next to hers. she is not disturbed.
the fuck furl does not bury the light, so the gloss erases her eyes.

let me look at you, look at that. look you, look that.
mmm. you are both my salve. let me munch your twattitty
in my brain. let me let you come to life.

he decides to name them both. the one with the face.
and the one with the twat and no pornface.

message from wolfgang

my mother left on the refrigerator

my father's back is a bracket. curled under all these
upright boys who trade baggies. a cane
won't help his posture.

in a dream i chase the motherfuckers down
with an ice cream truck. run over

the poor, the pop-eyed, the popsicle-eating, the twitchy and teenaged.

it's five in the morning on
a saturday. before the sun is even up
in winter,
                        the bracket passes.

my mouth is in shotguns,
barrels down their faces in blood over ice.
i talk about them like artificial flavor:
man-made, garden starved
high on barrels of empty sugar . . .

but when the phone rings,
i knock awake.

    (*call my house this early* . . .

their bodies look so little in red,
go so brown in the snow.

    pop, help me shovel the path, it's dark.

her handwriting has gotten arthritic. *5:32am* :
frank, wolfgang called. he's waiting on the corner.

six o'clock and the room arcs, half asleep.
he's out the door and god i hope,
god, i hope.

not now

sick, when the bend takes down the floor,

     and the country shakes.

sick : when drop settles rust in the shin. and has its way with you.

             the basement proselytizes. the concrete sluice.

sick when the names sound fade,

when faint. when fence looks up and takes on haint.

when sweat. when the stomach

folds and rolls up dough to throat.

           sick, can't play

or come out.

           can't speak, or touch tongue to pallet, can't mouth out.

sick or a moment in a prayer's position. hands to tile.

sick, and been down here for a while tasting grout,

craving the grit like a mow down for the mouth.

sick, and hanging on to sights on the corner wall, or is it floor that touched the ceiling

     and waned, pulled together to hover so

     like a low moan woman through bone.

must be dead, then, or the train come,

or the stool pigeon can't do shit, can't come home, can't stand up,

          can't strong enough to prove the numb set in, something chainsaw,

        something rip up, can't the tree cheeks, can't cow house, can't the wild hogs

       come sucking, come clicking across the tile. really can't shake it.

the cavity, the hung up with a choke rope.

sick, or the point at which

whistling would take on a mouth of blood, love a memory of umbilical needing to be cut. pushing blades to thrush, pumping mirrors to get to flood or stumps,

all river. take the run, rush narrow lips inside the elbow—
oh shit, sick. tie off. and spilling.
losing to patterned sap slowing milk from the bowel,

sauce thick with old vine wine, topped to blood. bent and coming up on dammit. tell them no, man. can't. can't make the trunk unburied. the head undead. the window slammed and

the iron split and foul. the nails, the asphalt and bile. the eggshells, dirty yolk.

the motrin cough. the salt wheeze. the carpet ants bent off topped up the windows til they crashed. now all the cops and daughters and silly curtains. thighs in drapes. wives with their mouths stuck open. tell them

can't. tell them sick now.

blanketface. mouth out. jawed.

eight days until your ashes turn one

i count how much it would take to make you live again. you know how your eyes ached and you would say *well maybe the glasses i get next year*, or the tomatoes sunk and you'd say *better soil next year* or the temperature dropped and you'd say *warmer next year*.

count. there were hundreds of pills and the reek of heroin, enough particles for a drop a day, a slipped afternoon, count them. high once—morning, once evening, tastes of gravy. reeks the same all night. smells the counted nickels, gathered dollar bills, scooped motrin along razor blade edges. count. the days between pall mall cigarettes, headaches, sex—did you? count those days. or count as the years ticked off where the grass didn't take, the garden—dust. our mother perched in her glasses, count

dropped stitches. wire frays. seeds to lay out for a dozen birds. thirty years, another day, the rotation of clock hand, wonder if she counted. or if you counted for her. how much drift and phoneme of garble, counted off in your nod

½ finished sentences, ellipses, ellipses, ellipses, stars. how many days did you track into some pore of your body that had been enumerated, renumbered

into an urn of dust. which in eight days will already be one. like one atom of your dilation

minus the ache.

roommates

the germ monster
from   under the scaffolding
        is in the cab now.
        we are drunk and way past queer

dirty free. he is bisexually gorgeous and

his stunning stitches
        hold
together
                the panels of his face.

he is blurred and tangle brown, some thing
to look forward to. get him home, horse mouthed and thick,
some could afford to watch, others to stand still and smoke.

tug at their nerdy pink shirts.
                        i'm so hot, he
offers to come back
no charge.   his odor

fucks up everything. his tongue

       folds gun clips
       into
my underwear

reeks long after the money exchange
he leaves

the iron gate open, the next day   is
                       mother's day.
my bra
carries the faded flagrance

the procession of
customers. my roommates

are out scrambling
for last minute
flowers.

in case there's trouble

blues for a mania

drab drab drab drab drip drab drab drab dark drab drab drab drab drab darb drab drab
drab drab crab drab drab drab bard drab drivel darb dripit drab drull drab drab drab drab
drab drab drunk drab drab darb drab dude drab drab dark drab drab drab drab drab arab
drab drab drum drab drab bark drab drab drap drab crab drab drab drab halo drab drab
drab drab drab drab crap drab drab drab drab drab dream drab drab drab drab drap drap
hrap drab drab drab drab drab drab dreg drab drab darn drab dram barb drab drab drab
drab drab drab drab drab drab drab odap drab drab dried drab drab drab drab drab drab
drab drab deaf drab drab carb drab darb drab drab drab damn drab drap drab drab dank
drab drag drab drar darb drab drab drar draf drab drab drab rag drab drag drinkit drabs
drab drab bard drab drab drab drab sag drab drab drab drab drab drab drab drab drain
drab junk drab drab gunk drab drab ark drab arch drab drab drill drab drab drab drama
drab drab karma drab drab urn drab drab drab drab drab ark drab drab darb drab yearn
drab drab mad drab drab breed drab drab drab drab drab drab drab drab drab drab drab
drab brand drab drab drab drab rain drab drab drab drab star drab you drab drab drab c
drab drab drab you can't drab drab drab drab drab sun drab drab drab drab drab drab
drab really drab drab drab drab drab arb drab you can't really dress up drab drab drab

anything

red is the mess

is the color of red ribbon, of red toast. is the crooked rubik's label falling off the rubik's cube. is the candle left to burn in the apartment. is not the flame. is not the smoke. is not the ride i take every morning on the bus downtown. red is the color of lips before the wind gets to them. is the color of sorrel too spicy sweet puckering white mouths. is the color of my scarf to set off all black. everyone wears all black. the bus is all black. is the color of my mother's lipstick

too red for my mouth. is the way she taught me how to whine. red is a balcony craving summer. it is a stiff need. red is the sky between haiti and baptist tongue. red is cheap ancho, peach. red is the dust fire, the gas leak, the monsoon crowding up under dead roses and ants. red is personal, blood. red is up under my father's veins. red is his red pop in ice cream tipping off the table. the big wheel i never got, the first garnet she pinned to my shirt. red is wedding cake, tom petty hustler. it's a website for cannibals, a black girl with an apple or a pomegranate.

red is kindergarten's favorite color and why. red is slaughterhouse. or it is beets. red is wine trickling down the pope's middle finger. red is a red cross coming too fast down a one-way street. red is my father's cigarette tipping off the table. red is the needle, the mess, the nod. red is his hair in sunshine. red looks dirtier in sunglasses, cute under lip gloss. red is embarrassing. is tucked in your lap. red is suicide. it clicks too many times when three falls short. it dances where the devil leaves off. its teeth are marred into every slave's back. speaking of which, it is southern mud. and hell. and a paper pouch for chopsticks. it's a sign of trains. a sign of trouble. it would be bad to find in milk. red is the pickup truck i wouldn't mind wrecking. it's your spiderman hung from the ceiling, upside down while i'm trying to write. it's the scent of kissing when we close our eyes.

katherine with the lazy eye.

short. and not a good poet.

this morning, i heard you were found in your mcdonald's uniform.

i heard it while i was visiting a lake town, where empty
woodsy highways turn into waterside drives.

i'd forgotten my toothbrush and was brushing my teeth with one finger.
a friend who didn't know you said he'd heard it like this: *you know katherine. short.*

with a lazy eye. poet. not a very good one. yeah, well she died. the blue on that lake
isn't so frank. it fogs off into the horizon like styrofoam. the

picnic tables full of white people. i ask them where the coffee is. they say at meijer.

i wonder if you thought about getting out of detroit. when you read at the open mic
you'd point across the street at mcdonald's and tell us to come see you.

katherine with the lazy eye. short and not a good poet, i guess i almost cried.
i don't know why, because i didn't like you. this is the first i remembered your name.

i didn't like how you followed around a married man. that your poems sucked
and that i figured they were all about the married man.

that sometimes you reminded me of myself, boy crazy. that sometimes
i think people just don't tell me that i'm kind of, well . . . slow.

katherine with the lazy eye, short. and not a good poet.
i didn't like that your lazy eye was always

looking at me. that you called me by my name. i didn't
like you, since the first time i saw you at mcdonald's.

you had a mop. and you were letting some homeless dude
flirt with you. i wondered then, if you thought that was the best

you could do. i wondered then
if it was.

katherine with the lazy eye, short. and not a good poet.
you were too silly to wind up dead in an abandoned building.

i didn't like you because, what was i supposed to tell you. what.
don't let them look at you like that, katherine. don't let them get you alone.

katherine with the lazy eye, short. and not a good poet. what
was i supposed to say to you, you don't get to laugh like that,

like nothing's gonna get you. not everyone
will forgive the slow girl. katherine with

the fucked up eye, short. poetry sucked, musta knew better. i avoided you
in the hallway. i avoided you in lunch line. i avoided you in the lake.

i avoided you. my lazy eye. katherine with one hideous eye, shit.
poetry for boys again, you should have been immune. you were supposed

to be a cartoon. your body was supposed to be as twisted as
it was gonna get. short. and not a good poet. katherine with

no eye no more. i avoided you. hated it when you said my name. i
really want to leave detroit. katherine with the lazy short.

not a good poet. and shit. somewhere someone has already asked
what was she like, and a woman has brought out her wallet and said

this is her. this is my beautiful baby.

i swear

allegiance

an angel would have to have crooked teeth. this would indicate dental problems the family couldn't afford to fix. an angel would need to be familiar with johnson & johnson and cocoa butter. could explain the taste of powdered eggs. an angel would have to know when to shut the fuck up. an angel would not come drunk on vodka and would prefer gin filthy. it's hard to tell which angels know how to make chitterlings, but a good angel would not mind you asking.

an east side angel would know how to rig the gas meter without alerting d.t.e. an angel could pick a good wine from the orange price tag stickers at the liquor store. a detroit angel will know where to get a monthly bus card. a city angel will know where the river's current means jumping in is really suicide. a detroit angel could tell you where you can use a public computer. an archangel could tell you where to find one all night.

any angel would bring a new lexicon. a city angel would mold a wall of ears because there's too much bullshit for two. a detroit angel would take all this loose religious fervor and build us a jesus. an angel would let you take cuts. an east side angel would let you finish your sentence. any angel would help you pack your shit when it's time to move. an angel will give you back your lost pen. an east side angel has a spot for you on their porch. most angels can fuck. some angels wear metal. an east side angel knows that girls like the taste of pillows, even if they don't talk about it.

a detroit angel will give you three feet of personal space at the bus stop. any angel will call you first after your date. an angel will often call you an angel. too many angels smoke. some angels let their bodies go. an angel put his weight on you. an angel limber in clouds. an angel will pick up the coat you dropped. an east side angel never asks you for cash. a detroit angel has never had to use a gun. a city angel, something dark around the eyes. shit talking, lunar mouthed angel. crazy angel with a chipped bone limp. bipolar angel with a snapped wing shoulder. quiet angel, sit with you all night. an east side angel can read your mind. narcissist angel, icarus angel. lush angel picking its hair up off the floor. screeching vocalist violet, improv dead horns overdose. angels addicted to addict angels. needs a punch to feel it angel. no one hears the angel scream. an angel takes in the groceries, climbs the stairs. bad knee angels. angels subtle. no one gets the subtle angel.

angels wear nightgowns stuck in their butts. angels' grey hair don't age them right. angels' black pool around the eyes. angels mean suicide and it comes out shapes. angels know how to fight off the cops. angels offer you coffee. offer you coffee. angels might have taken back everything they're giving you now. angels bloody lip. angels bashed in heads. angels never broke a bone, don't need stitches. offer you coffee, offer you coffee. east side angels don't ever change, still look the same. east side angels, same address. east side angels on the sideline in case the blows are too bloody. detroit angels stay close to home, close to mama. east side angels gaps in their teeth. detroit angels wings stuck in detroit. angels pace their east side floor. angels pack their wings in luggage. angels lock their halos in emergency glass, in case there's trouble.

acknowledgments

Thanks to the following journals in which some of these poems originally appeared:

Boxcar: "i live in detroit"; *ElevenEleven*: "between old trees," "confessional poetry," "(i belong to that voice. it owns what i breathe.)," "message from wolfgang my mother left on the refrigerator"; *Torch*: "to the man on the bus"; *Mead Magazine*: "sift," "another finger for the wound"; *Michigan Quarterly Review*: "what you'd find buried under charles f. kettering sr. high school"; *Rattle*: "katherine with the lazy eye. short. and not a good poet." An earlier version of "you, old meany" appeared in the chapbook *between old trees*. An earlier version of "flashes—cyan / magenta / yellow" appeared in *Voices Rising: Celebrating 20 Years of Black LGBT Writing*.

Thanks to Cave Canem, the Provincetown Fine Arts Work Center, the University of Michigan MFA Creative Writing Department, InsideOut Literary Arts, and Callaloo for support of this work and my writing process. Much love to all the people who made WriteWordWrightNow—right then. Thanks to Mary Jo Firth's writing circle in the faraway library. A special thanks to David Blair, Tommye Blount, Andrew Chanse, Nandi Comer, Garrett DeVoe, Eric Dilworth, Demetrius F. Dumas, Lavone Forbes, Vievee Francis, Ross Gay, George Henry, Jamaal May, Shawn Nicholson, Gregory Pardlo, Jeff Perlstein, Scheherazade Parrish, Lawrence Peterson, Jamaul Roots, Brandon Som, and Scott Winn for all the years of support that went into this first book.

Printed in the USA
CPSIA information can be obtained
at www.ICGtesting.com
LVHW081429270924
791621LV00055B/558